How To Start A Business

5 Simple and Easy Steps To Start Your Business and Be Successful

Table of Contents

Introduction

Have you ever wanted a comprehensive blueprint on how exactly it is that one sets up a successful business? Well you're in the right place. Most books only give a snippet of all the steps involved. What happens there, is that by the time we get to the end of the book, we are still left pretty clueless as to what the next step should be. This book is much more solution based. It is packed with all the information that you really need to build a successful business from the ground up. By the time you get to the end of this book, you will be well equipped to hit the ground running and get started on building your empire.

Being an entrepreneur and owning your own business can be very rewarding. It can make you a billionaire and give you freedom to work on your own time but it also has a various elements to it that can knock the wind out of you if you are not prepared which is why I wrote this book. It will outline the steps to take and things to look out for so that you can save yourself some expensive mistakes that a lot of entrepreneurs tend to make.

In this book, we will cover everything from choosing a business, building your team, and getting funding, to marketing your business and scaling your business for long term success and achieving time freedom. It is jam-pack with tips and techniques for successful entrepreneurship, while being short enough to be an easy read. We will not only look at how to start a successful business, but also how to sustain it so that it will last and produce revenue for you and your family for generations to come.

We will discuss beyond the 'what' and look at the 'how' and 'why' certain actions need to be taken. Regardless of what business you're in, somethings are standard right across the board. Let's get rid of all the blur and guesswork involved in starting a business.

This book will knock your socks off with all the things that didn't know about business success. This book is filled with relevant information (no beating around the bush) to get you from A to Z in the business that you love!

Thanks again for downloading this book, I hope you enjoy it and leave your honest review at the end. Enjoy!

Chapter 1: Choose Your Business Idea

Coming up with a business idea or choosing the type of business you want to build is the obvious first step right? Some will tell you to follow your passion and some will tell you to copy the actions of a billionaire business owner. I say follow your gut, which is essentially the same thing as follow your passion. Jay Z once said "stick to the things that you understand; the things that are true to you". That is one of the greatest pieces of advice that you will ever get in business. Many people are tempted to jump on what looks trendy, or what's making money today. What usually happens from there is, they invest loads of time and money, only to realize a couple months later that it's not for them.

There are trillions of business ideas out there that are making money. Never do something because its trendy or it "makes money". Do it because it is true to you and true to what you stand for. So how exactly do you pick or create the best business idea?

Answer these questions

What are you passionate about? - This could be anything from swimming to wine tasting. Your passion is anything that you would do on a regular basis even if you never ever get paid a dollar to do it.

What problem will your business solve? -

Many people don't know this but the essence of any business is that it solves some sort of problem. A good bakery solves the problem of there being no attractive pastries available in that area. A financial institution solves the problem of people no longer having to walk around with large sums of cash. It also allows people to do business with other people from all over the world. Your business must solve a problem for it to stay relevant and for customers to stay loyal. Businesses based on passion alone, only last for so long.

Is there a particular clientele/customer base that you wish to have? - This refers mainly to the income bracket that your target customers fall in. Some people fear that identifying a specific target market will cause you to lose out on business, but it is actually the other way around. Trying to sell to everyone from every income bracket and background is a recipe for disaster. People buy things that they feel cater to their specific needs, and customers are

turned off by "one size fits all" type of businesses. Narrow your target market down to a specific group and aim to be the best in that area. An example of a target market is: Athletic men between the ages of 21 and 35 living in an English speaking western country making between USD$25,000 and $40,000 per year. It gives a clear picture of who your product is aimed at.

How much money and time are you willing to invest? – This is the big one. There are businesses that may cost millions to start, some may cost a couple hundred dollars and some you can start at no cost to you at all. I don't want you to limit your beliefs of what you think is possible for you, but it is important to get your facts and finances straight before diving in. Definitely, be realistic about how much it is going to cost to start your business. Always overestimate your expenses and underestimate your revenues to set realistic expectations. Now, notice I made mention of time as well. This is where many may fall down. Even with the best equipment and overflowing resources, you must put in the time and possess the will to get your ideas off the ground. You can start a business with no money, but you have to be willing to put in the time in order to attain success.

Pursue the options

After answering the questions above, you should have an idea of at least the industry that you want to be in; whether it's Television,

Technology, Food, Health, or something else. The next step is to pursue your options. Get a paper and pen and flesh out the ideas. If you are going to create or innovate something, list out all the elements that the business will have, choose a name, and make a list of things that you will accomplish with this business.

If you are going the route of reinventing a business idea that already exists, then you have a slight advantage. The first thing that you need to do is research. Go on google or yellow pages, and look up all the different businesses that are in that industry to help you elaborate on your idea. The next thing that you'll want to do is find out which company is #1 in that industry.

Pick it apart! That is your competition. If you are going to aim at all, then aim high, so get a paper and pen and write down all the things that you would change about the company. Then write down all the things that you like about the company. You now have a blueprint to build your company, and make it better than your competitor. It will take some time to get where they are, but at least with this blueprint, you may avoid some mistakes that they endured.

Test the waters

Doing this step will save you lots of headaches and money. If your business is based on a product, create some prototype of your product or samples, and send it out into the market. To incentivize customers to try it, give the samples away free or at a highly reduced cost in exchange for their opinion and suggestions. This is market research and it is invaluable to the success of your business. Think about it like this. You could do a full scale production and create a product that the market does not want, and end up losing a lot of time and money, OR you can do a very small scale production to produce samples that customers can test and allow yourself to make necessary changes, or move on to a better idea. No matter how much you and your mom love your business idea, keep in mind, who will actually be buying your product to make you rich. Customers! You are literally at the mercy of your consumers so invest the time and money to do the necessary research before jumping in.

If your business is a service then you clearly can't make samples, but what you can do, is offer your services free of charge in exchange for reviews or just to get the word out that you're on the verge of starting a business. Nothing travels faster than word of mouth, and potential customers trust what their friends say more than what a TV Ad says, so offering your services for free can really pay off and give you that real push to get your business going.

Chapter 2: Find the Right Business Partner and Build Your Team

I'm sure you've heard the saying "No man is an island" many times before. This is very true for building a business, let alone a wildly successful business. You can be the main source of ideas, or the executive decision maker, but at some point you are going to need some help. The solution lies in finding the right business partner. You can have one or more business partners. The number of persons you choose does not matter even half as much as the kind of person that you choose. So how does one find the right kind of business partner to ensure the business' success? Here are a few guidelines to go by:

Test the chemistry before signing on the dotted line

Not every business pairing will have this luxury but as much as is possible, spend some time working with your potential business partner before you make things official. Sounds like a marriage? Well it kind of is. You will have to make important decisions with this person, so you need to consider all the factors involved.

Someone may look fabulous on paper but in person, the chemistry just is not there. Lack of genuine chemistry between business partners can cause unrepairable damage and cause the business to fail. As the owner of the business, you have to first play the role of a scout. Go to business functions and conferences, and meet new people who are like-minded. Then, narrow the prospects. Reach out to the top three, or maybe just the one that stands out to you the most, and create a project to work on together.

Going to lunch together and working together are two different things, so work on a simple project together as a test run, to give you a preview of working with the person permanently. Hopefully all goes well and you can start working together on a permanent basis. If things don't go so well, keep looking. This is a big deal so do not settle. Also remember when things become more permanent, put everything in writing, in a contract to save yourself some legal trouble should things go south.

Spend some quality time together

Testing the chemistry was more about the business relationship but since this is a long-term situation, you are going to want build a genuine friendship with this person. A good way to develop a friendship with someone is to do extracurricular activities together. Go hiking, fishing, exercising or shopping. Have occasional lunch meetings together to build that bond that great business partners have.

This will help you understand the other person more. You can get insight into their family life and childhood to get a better understanding of why they think the way that they do, and what differences/similarities that you may have. This information will come in handy during the decision-making process or help you work out any disputes that arise.

There is so much more to a person than what meets the eye. I'm sure you would even agree that the same is true about yourself. Next to your family, no one understands you like your closest friends. Although it is often said to never mix fun and business, this is the one exception to that rule.

Ensure that you have the same values but different skill sets

Values are very important in business partners because it is the core of the decisions that they make. Do they always engage in ethical practices? Or do they take the short cut and bend the rules sometimes? Which of the two do you wish to be associated with? You want to make sure that your "normal" is similar to their "normal" so if you get to work at 7am sharp every morning ready to work, does your business partner do the same? And how does that affect your productivity as a team.

There are some fundamentals that must be the same or similar between you and your business partner to ensure the highest level of productivity. Your skills however, should not be the same. The whole point of having a business partner, is that he/she can bring something to the table that you can't.

Perfect example of this is Steve Jobs and Steve Wozniak of Apple. Both were key to the creation of Apple but the reason that their partnership worked was because they each brought something different to the table. Wozniak was a phenomenal coder. He understood programming and coding in a way that Apple benefited greatly from. Jobs was an extraordinary, creative businessman. Jobs understood design and marketing in a way that was equally as important. The symmetry of the two skills is what made that business partnership such a successful one.

Outline a clear decision making process

As stated before, when you take on a business partner, you will have to start making all the important decisions together. No longer can it be "my way or the highway". Making decisions with someone else can be a pain in the rear, even with someone who has the same values as you, so it is crucial that you outline a decision making process with your business partners, where one person is not allowed to take action without the consent of the other. Make sure that it is always a team effort.

Chapter 3: Getting Funding

Funding is essential to any business. It could be a small amount or a large sum but the process is pretty standard. If you are setting up a small, one-man-show kind of business, then you can probably access funding privately from your family or friends but if you have a big business idea or wish to scale up your current business, this chapter will be especially helpful to you. So let's get into it and look at some of the most effective ways to get funding for your business.

Crowdfunding

This is one of the newer ways to access funding for your business. Through the internet, you now have access to hundreds and maybe even thousands of potential investors through crowdfunding websites. These websites may follow different models.

The first one is the donation model, which has been around for years. This is where people donate money in small increments to a project or business which they believe is moral and overall good for the community. An example of this is a site call gofundme.com.

The second model is the pre-order model. This is when people make online pledges during a campaign or pre-buy the product for later delivery. A popular website using this model is kickstarter.com.

The third is the reward-based model where investors just help voluntarily, and immediately receive a reward for doing so. The perfect example of this is indiegogo.com.

Finally, there is the equity model which is also relatively new. This is when large numbers of people online can invest in a start-up business in small amounts. They can expect to receive dividends or an appreciation on their investment. Crowdfunding revenues reportedly topped $2 billion USD in 2014, so it is definitely an option worth looking into.

Venture Capitalists and Angel Investors

A venture capitalist is usually a firm that invests money in a startup business or businesses that want to expand. They typically receive higher returns on their investments doing this, than they would on other traditional forms of investing. You can go to a Venture Capital firm or an Angel Investor to pitch your idea. An angel investor is very similar to venture capitalists but an angel investor is usually just one person who has a large sum of disposable income that they would like to invest in a startup business, in return for part ownership of the business. Angel investors usually act as silent partners, meaning they get a cut of the profits, but they don't particularly concern themselves with the day to day operations of the business.

When attempting to attain funding from a venture capital firm or an angel investor, the best piece of advice is to show your true personality. They might think that your business idea is not the best, but if they like you and see your potential, they will give you the money that you need. Most people invest in people, not businesses, so work on your winning personality and you should be good to go.

Small Business Loans

This is usually a person's first thought when they think of getting money to start a business, but compared to the previous two options, a small business is the most complicated and perhaps the most difficult to attain. The thing is, start-up businesses are often see as risky investments, because so many of them fail per year and there is absolutely no guarantee of success. Banks are just not as willing to take that kind of risk that individual investors would, especially if you have no collateral (car, house, or another business).

If you do have collateral however, a small business loan may actually be a good option for you. Why? Because you don't have to give them any gift or part ownership in return for the loan. All you have to do, is pay the loan back at their stated interest rate. You can spread this payback period over a number of years or pay it off in a matter of months. It is all up to you. Do your research to find the bank with the lowest interest rate, and ensure that you have your finances in order because your credit score along with valid collateral, are big deciding factors in whether you are approved or declined for the loan.

Chapter 4: How To Market Your Business

No matter what type of business you are in or where you are in life, this chapter is crucial for you to grasp. First let us look at what marketing really is? A short and simple definition is: Marketing is the action of promoting and selling a good or service. Let us break that down and first look at selling.

The truth is, that selling is a part of our daily lives, whether or not we are dealing with business, and those who sell well, tend to progress faster. Think about it. A man who asks a woman out on a date has to sell her the idea of going out with him. A little girl who wants a new puppy has to sell her parents on the idea of why she deserves to have it. A business owner has to sell the value of his product to his customers. You can't escape selling, so you might as well master it.

Now selling by itself can sometimes come across as aggressive, depending on your style. This is where promotion comes in and promotion is all about raising public awareness. The marriage of selling and promotion is what creates marketing. You have to strategize your marketing to get your brand seen, remembered and to foster a constant flow of customers. Let's look at some of the most effective marketing strategies:

Website or Blog

These days, for a business to be successful, you must have an online presence. A website should be the hub of your online presence, because the first thing that someone will do when they find out about your business, is Google it. You want to ensure that what they find, will solidify their trust in the brand and also promote the brand in a positive light.

A blog is also a great way to stay relevant and constantly update your website with new content. You can set up a website and/or blog using a hosting site like Hostgator or Bluehost and sync it with Wordpress software. That can be a bit technical however, so sites such as Blogger, Wix.com and Squarespace are some other easy, user-friendly options.

Link your blog and all your social media account back to your website so that customers will have the convenience of finding everything in one place. Everybody loves convenience!

Social Media

Speaking of social media, this is also crucial in the marketing strategy of your business in this content-sharing age. People will also search for brand on their favorite social media platforms like Facebook, Twitter, Instagram, and Pinterest. You need to know how to effectively use each to get the optimal benefit.

Twitter is used for sharing short content and links, and is perhaps the most interactive platform. Spend time here replying to as many people as possible and engage in conversations using trending hashtags. This will bring targeted attention to you and your brand. Facebook is best for sharing pictures and larger amounts of content because unlike Twitter, Facebook has no word limit on each post. Pinterest is a good way to bring attention to your blog by posting attractive pictures. Don't just post your content however. Engage with the community by repining from other people's boards.

Instagram is big on hashtags. You can't link any websites or blogs to your posts here, so the best way to market your business here is to promote events and items with attractive images. Treat Instagram as how you would treat print advertising. There are new forms of social media coming out every year so stay current and join those which are relevant to you and your business.

Email Marketing

It is a super effective way of staying in touch with customers on a regular basis. Have customers sign up their name and email address when they buy from you or visit your website. It can be a physical form or the more convenient online form.

Have these email addresses transferred to email marketing service such as MailChimp or Aweber and send them a newsletter or update every month or week. You can also use email marketing to update them on product launches and promotions. This way, your brand never leaves the mind of the customer and they are inclined to repurchase or refer a friend.

Business Cards

The good old business card has definitely stood the test of time. With all the technology that surrounds us, many people neglect the power of tangible forms of marketing such as promotional pens/keychains, flyers and business cards. Even if you do away with the first three, a business card is essential. It should include your name, telephone number, email address, website and any other relevant contact information. Your business card should reflect you and your business well. Get creative to make your card memorable, but keep it professional so that they take you seriously.

Socialize

It is probably the best kept secret that if you hang around influential people, then some of their influence will rub off on you. There was a scientific study that showed that when a photo of a famous person was placed beside the photo of a non-famous person, the non-famous person was thought to be more famous than they actually were. This can actually work to your favor if you are simply even seen with the big players in your industry. The buzz will spread about who you are and what you do. That being said, when out and about, be cognizant of what you are doing. You can have fun, but always represent your brand well. Remember, people care more about the person behind the business than about the business itself.

Advertise

There are so many ways to advertise a business. You can advertise on television, billboards, flyers, radio, magazines, blogs, social media ads and the list goes on. The gold however is in choosing which platforms are most effective for your specific business. My biggest suggestion would be to go online first.

It is as simple as starting a Google Adsense account and creating an ad that will show up on relevant sites. When someone discovers a new business, the first thing that they do is look it up on the internet and ecommerce is steadily growing. Advertising on the internet is very cost effective and just makes the most sense.

Once you have a bigger budget then delve into television ads and other platforms.

Chapter 5: Scale Up and Expand Your Business

Scaling up your business or expansion should be in your thoughts with every move that you make in the business. Every time you have an important decision to make, ask yourself, "How is this going to benefit the business in the long term?" Your business should be constant growth and progression or one day everything will come to a dead end, so think "Expansion" from the very beginning.

The statistics of the number of start-up businesses that fail within one year of operation is staggering. It is as much as 80% and I believe that this happens because business owners do not scale up when they should. Why? They are either afraid or genuinely don't know how to expand. If fear is the reason, that boils down to self-belief and believing that your business is destined for greatness even when no one else believes it.

If you don't look into expansion because you don't know how... well we're going to cover that in this chapter so pay close attention.

There are five steps involved in expanding your business so let's look at each step individually.

Dream Big and Put It Into Action

Your vision for your business should be massive from the get go if you intend to be the owner of a wildly successful business. It is also important to note that dreaming alone is not going to get you any further today than you were yesterday. It is the action that follows the dreaming, that actually makes the difference. Any great business owner or anyone who has "made it" in the eyes of society, started with a dream or a thought that it was possible.

The best strategy for brainstorming and figuring out what your goals for the business are, is to write it down. Pen to paper is tried and true, to help you think clearly. Write down your goals for the next year, 5 years and then 10 years. This helps you to then figure out what daily actions you need to take to achieve those goals.

The next step is to take daily action towards achieving your goals. This is just as important as writing them down. Success rarely every happens overnight. It is the accumulation or taking necessary steps forward, day after day, over a sustained period of time.

Work on Your Business, Not In Your Business

This could easily be one of the biggest mistakes that new entrepreneurs tend to make. Many people think that starting their business means that they have to do everything themselves for it to be done right. This is so far from the truth, and over time it causes the entrepreneur to feel burnt out before they even get to make the big bucks. The truth is that nobody is amazing at everything, much as we love to believe otherwise.

Here is an example of what I mean. Jane may be an amazing baker but she is just not that great at marketing and social media. It also takes up a lot of her time. Initially she is a one-woman-show. She spends her days baking for customers and then tries to catch up on social media at the end of the day, but no one likes her posts or replies to her tweets. She feels overwhelmed and hires a marketing manager, John for the bakery. Now she can focus on what she really loves, which is baking and she leaves social media and marketing to John.

Why would you do everything yourself, when you can hire someone else to do it for you? The next step for Jane would be to hire assistant bakers as well so that she can bake when she wants to, rather than because she has to. She can take vacations because the business can now operate even if she is not there. Jane can then look into scaling up and expanding the business' reach. She is now working ON her business rather than IN her business.

Get Funding For Expansion

Contrary to popular belief, most businesses are not self-funded. It may seem difficult at first to access external funding but with persistence it is possible. When thinking about expansion, funding is necessary because unless you run a $1 million company, using the company's revenues for expansion purposes is very risky.

It is best to either make an arrangement with a venture capitalist or take a loan that you can pay back over a stretch of time. In many cases, funding for expansion usually pays for itself once the work is done. As Mark Cuban would say "Sales solve everything".

Build Up Your Public Persona

The world of commerce is moving away from being business-to-business or business-toconsumer. It is more of a people-to-people world now. With the new advancements in technology and the increased popularity to share everything through social media, consumers are no longer satisfied with just knowing the name of the brand. They want to know who is behind the brand.

Building your public persona is not only good for your current company but if done correctly, it can set you up for a head start in any other business that you plan to start in the future. The best examples of this include the likes of Steve Jobs, Jay Z and Mark Cuban. In the case of Steve Jobs, he is arguably more popular than the Apple brand itself, and this worked in his favor. Jay Z has diversified in business much more than Jobs, but the principle still applies. Any business he starts or becomes a part of automatically gains some level of credibility, because of his past successes. The same can be said for Mark Cuban.

So how do you apply this principle to your own life and business? In this digital age, anyone can start a blog or website. This is a very effective way to establish yourself as an expert in your preferred niche. Write valuable content and maintain a presence on social media. If you're up for it, YouTube is also an excellent platform to get your voice heard.

Scaling up your business is as mentioned before, necessary if you have your eyes on the big prize. There is hard work involved but following these tried and true tips will take you and your business to the next level.

Conclusion

Thank you again for downloading this book! *How To Start A Business* was written to give new and established entrepreneurs a comprehensive guide to having success in their specific businesses. This book has cut out a lot of the guess work that many people face when wanting to take that leap to bring their idea to life, or to simply work for themselves. Contrary to popular belief, business is kind of like a game that you can win, and it is not as complicated as some might have you believe. This book has proven just that.

We covered the strategies to choosing a business idea, finding a reliable business partner/team, getting access to funding, marketing your business and ultimately expanding and scaling up your business. The overall most important topics were chosen for this book to give a full picture of what you need to build a successful business from scratch.

My goal with this book is to provide readers with a convenient and comprehensive book of all the information needed to start a successful business, and prevent the confusion and unnecessary information that I had to sift through when building my first two companies. I hope you learned all the information and strategies that you always wanted to know. Now you can implement what you read from this book into your business.

My wish for you is that you have a very successful life and business and share what you know to make the journey easier for someone else.